C000051079

Motivate You

AN INSPIRATIONAL BOOK

ANNAKAYE MILLER

Copyright © 2022 Annakaye Miller

ISBN:
978-1-952874-63-5 (paperback)
978-1-952874-64-2 (ebook)

All rights reserved. No part of this publication may be reproduced, stored in a retrieval system, or transmitted in any form or by any means - electronic, mechanical, photocopy, recording, scanning, or other – except for brief quotations in critical reviews or articles, without the prior written permission of the publisher.

Published by:

 OMNIBOOK Co.

OMNIBOOK CO.
99 Wall Street, Suite 118
New York, NY 10005
USA
+1-866-216-9965
www.omnibookcompany.com

For e-book purchase: Kindle on Amazon, Barnes and Noble
Book purchase: Amazon.com, Barnes & Noble, and
www.omnibookcompany.com

Omnibook titles may be purchased in bulk for educational, business, fund-raising, or sales promotional use. For more information please e-mail info@omnibookcompany.com

CONTENTS

EXISTENCE

Thank you, God,
for creating us because without you,
we wouldn't exist.

Thank you, God,
for creating all the creatures because without you,
they wouldn't exist.

Thank you, God,
for creating this world because without you,
we wouldn't be in it.

Thank you, God,
because without you,
there is no us.

Thank you, God,
for this beautiful life, because without it,
we are nothing.

Thank you, God,
for everything you do,
we really appreciate you.

BEAUTIFULLY MADE

I believe you are beautifully made by God,
yes indeed, unique in your own special ways, just let it be.
Why worry about your flaws, no one is perfect,
even the ones who look physically perfect
on the outside have flaws deep within, you just can't see it.
Don't try to change for anyone,
because you are beautifully made by God.

LOVE YOURSELF

Love yourself,
even when people think the worse of you.

Love yourself,
because you are beautiful inside and out.

Love yourself,
because God made you in His image
and He is beautifully divine.

Love yourself,
because no one else can love you the way you love YOU.

Love yourself,
because you are amazing
and you deserve the best in this world.

Love yourself,
because you are you and no one else can ever be you.

Love yourself,
because you are truly a blessing from God
and He made you just the way you are.

PHENOMENAL

You are phenomenal, smart, and extraordinary. These are just some of the words that describe you, full of energy and outspoken. Yes, I'm describing you! Look in the mirror gorgeous! Yes, I'm talking to you. Listen to these words I am saying to you, you are loved, you are important, you are amazing, and you are enough. So lift that chin up and let people see your beautiful smile.

SPECIAL

Special, you are, yes indeed,
God made you just for me.
Beautiful eyes just so sweet,
make you fall into a dream.
Beautiful face let me see,
oh I could stare at you all day, just let me be.
Beautiful body now I see,
why they are turning their heads just to see.
Beautiful mind, beautiful being,
continue to be the best they see.

THE ONE OF MY DREAMS

Special you are to me; you'll always be the one of my dreams.
The way you love me it's so real. Please don't ever leave me.
Special you are just hold me close and never let me go.
Special you are and special you'll be in my life forever.

PROUD TO BE YOU

Proud to be you, because in your eyes,
you're beautiful from head to toe.
Proud to be you, because you're not perfect and nobody is.
Proud to be you, even though people dislike you,
when they never even get a chance to know you.
Proud to be you, even when things don't work out the way it's supposed to.
Proud to be you because there's no one else like you.

SHOW OUT

Show out! Because your inner beauty lies within, something your physical beauty would never understand.

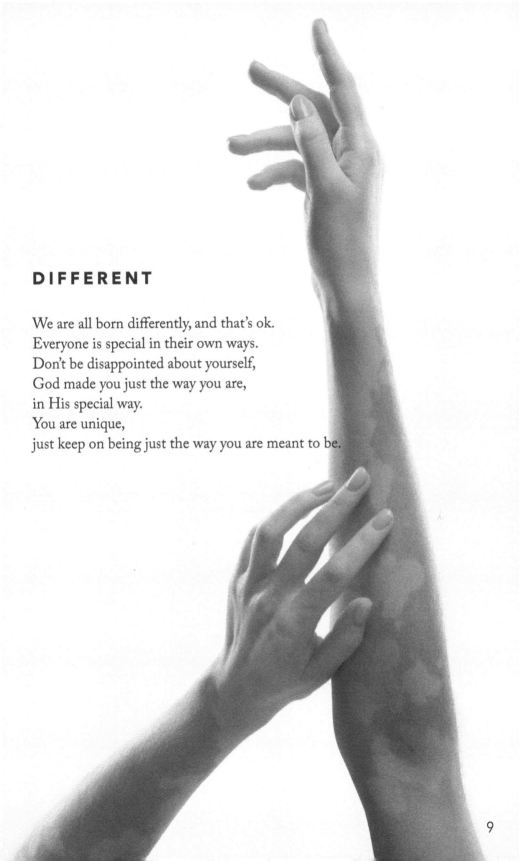

DIFFERENT

We are all born differently, and that's ok.
Everyone is special in their own ways.
Don't be disappointed about yourself,
God made you just the way you are,
in His special way.
You are unique,
just keep on being just the way you are meant to be.

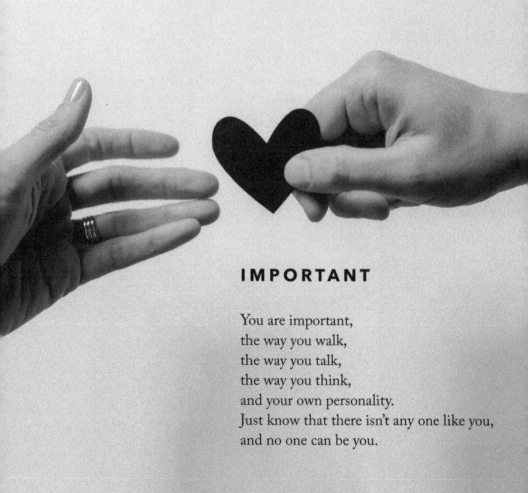

IMPORTANT

You are important,
the way you walk,
the way you talk,
the way you think,
and your own personality.
Just know that there isn't any one like you,
and no one can be you.

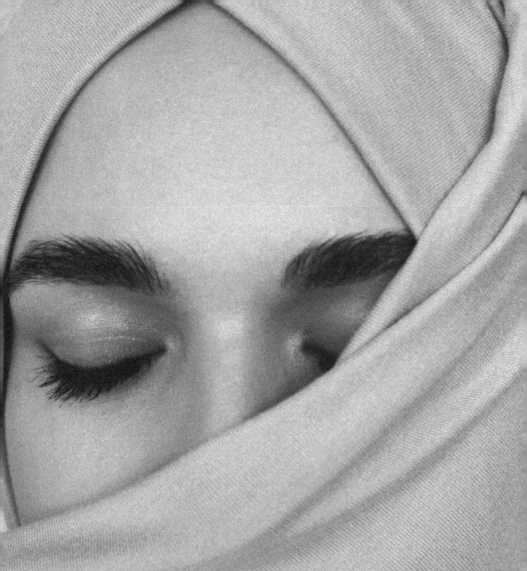

BEAUTY FROM WITHIN

The genuine radiance of beauty lies from within.
The beauty with a pure heart that's within.
The beauty so kind and gentle that treats people right,
with that tender caring heart, oh how priceless that is.
The beauty that's good and stands out,
so noticeable everyone can see.
If you got that beauty, physically and within,
then you are surely a true beauty that outshines all.
The best there is.

CONFIDENCE

Own it! Don't be afraid to be different.
You are born to stand out, that's why each person is different.
Keep owning your confidence, you don't have to fit in.
Just stand out and be confident because there is no one like you.

THE BEST

Make the best of it, that's all we can do.
We got to live and be who you truly are.
Look within your soul so deep,
and bring out the beautiful being you are to be.
Live and be happy, live and be free.
Don't ever fear what's meant to be.
Love and strive to the top,
because you got to make the best of what you got.

THE GUY YOU WANT

The guy you want, hmmm,
he is exactly what you're looking for,
sexy, handsome, and smart.
The guy of your dreams.
The way he walks,
the way he talks. OMG!
The smell of his perfume
will drive you insane.
If only he could look your way,
your life would be complete.
The only problem is,
he's just not into you.

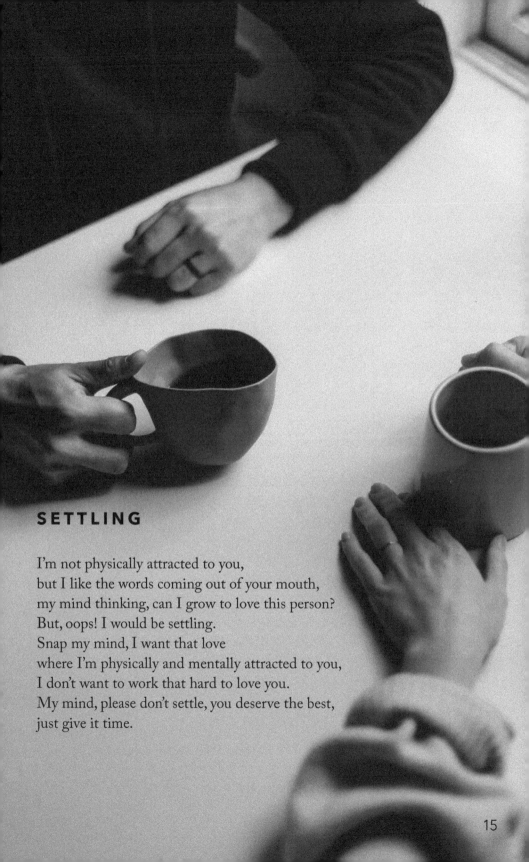

SETTLING

I'm not physically attracted to you,
but I like the words coming out of your mouth,
my mind thinking, can I grow to love this person?
But, oops! I would be settling.
Snap my mind, I want that love
where I'm physically and mentally attracted to you,
I don't want to work that hard to love you.
My mind, please don't settle, you deserve the best,
just give it time.

CONNECTION

I want that connection where a day won't pass
without you thinking of me.
A connection even if something's wrong,
you know without me saying anything.
A connection where I know you got me
and nothing else matters.
A connection so deep that even if you're hurting,
I'm hurting too because I can't bear to see you in pain.
A connection so strong not even a thunderstorm can't tear it apart.
A connection if you're gone for a day,
I miss you so much because I can't wait to see your face.
I want that connection, where you can't see your life without me in it.

TRUE LOVE

The day I met you,
my heart melted,
your eyes,
your nose,
your mouth,
so beautiful.
The way I love you,
they say, it's love at first sight
but for me,
it was the only true love I know,
my beautiful child.
I love you.

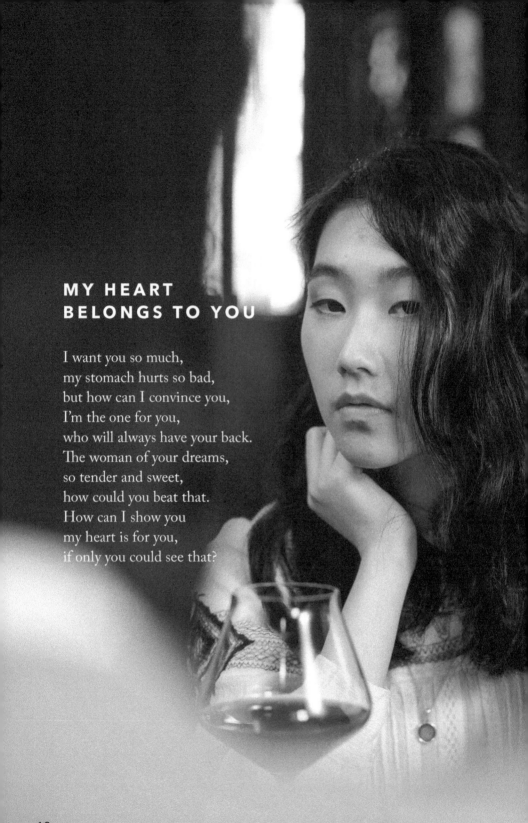

MY HEART
BELONGS TO YOU

I want you so much,
my stomach hurts so bad,
but how can I convince you,
I'm the one for you,
who will always have your back.
The woman of your dreams,
so tender and sweet,
how could you beat that.
How can I show you
my heart is for you,
if only you could see that?

I PROMISE YOU

I'll be there for you through good times and bad.
I'll take care of you, I promise you that.

WISHING YOU WERE MINE

Infatuated with your beauty, oh divine.
You are really one of a kind.
I believe you were first in line,
so God took his time
and made you so divine.
Lusting for you,
oh what can I do,
just wishing one day you'll be mine.

SO INTO YOU

Into you, I'm so into you.
I'm thinking of you every single day.
I like your style; you make me smile.
Oh, the thoughts that flow through my brain.
Into you, just let me, be with you so I can see your gorgeous face.
The way we vibe, oh darling you are fine, just like a glass of wine.
Oh, please be into me, like I'm into you.

SECRET ADMIRER

Looking at you every day
makes me go into a happy place.
Thinking, if you only knew
how much I'm into you.
Wishing one day you'll be mine.
Even though I'll never get that chance
because someone already found you first.
The only thing I can do
Is look at you each day,
and continue to be
your secret admirer.

YOUR GRACE

Knock, knock, guess who is here,
it's your beauty and grace joining near.
Oh, what a pleasure to grace your presence so near.
I would climb a mountain to see your grace.
Knock, knock guess who is here,
it's your beautiful mind that draws me near.
The way you think it's extraordinary.
Oh, what a pleasure to be around your intelligent grace.
Knock, knock it's your beautiful spirit coming my way.
The way you're so caring and loving will make anyone feel better.
Oh, what a pleasure to be around with such a beautiful being.
Thank you for gracing me with your presence, it was such a delight.

SWEET

You're so sweet every time I look at you, you give me a toothache.
So sweet not even a candy can compete with your sweetness.
You're so sweet you could turn something sour into sweet.
Sweet because your sweetness is overwhelming,
it's giving me a headache I'm willing to bear.
Sweet just stay exactly the way you are,
no need to argue, because you are too sweet for me
to even open my mouth to say anything to upset you.
Sweet, I will stick with you because, I rather have you than nothing else.

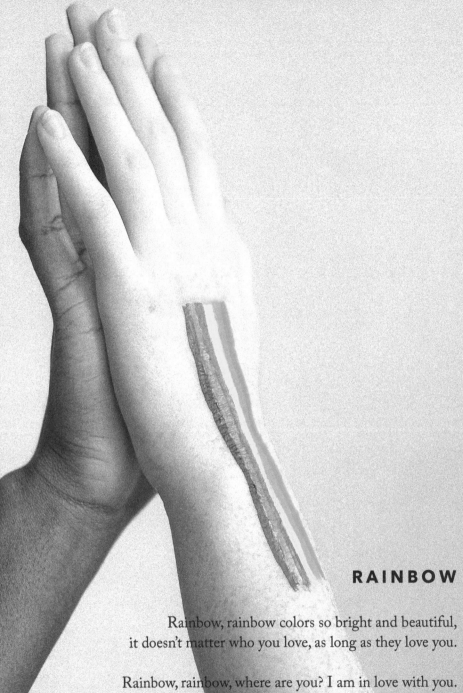

RAINBOW

Rainbow, rainbow colors so bright and beautiful,
it doesn't matter who you love, as long as they love you.

Rainbow, rainbow, where are you? I am in love with you.
No matter what color, I love you, and because you love me too.
Ain't no one going to keep us away. Love has no shape nor form.
You are the one, and this is true because you are beautiful in every way.

Rainbow, rainbow don't you change because I will never stop loving you.

SUPPORT

When you have someone that gives you the support you need. That's so awesome, someone who sticks with you and pushes you to do your best and never gives up on you. Someone you can turn to when the roads get bumpy, and you feel like giving up. Someone to comfort and take care of you if you are not feeling well. Someone, who, when you're sad will try their best to cheer you up because they hate it when you are sad. Someone who loves your flaws and appreciates you, for just the way you are. Someone who got you and you could never doubt that, because they'll always have your back, and you know that.

THE FEELING YOU GIVE ME

Loving you each day,
it's a feeling I can't describe,
the feeling I'm having
explodes my mind,
I thank God I met you,
every single day,
the way you treat me,
with so much respect.
The love you show me
makes me feel so blessed.

WHISPER

Whisper with that voice so tender
that calms me down in just a second.
Whisper with your voice so sweet
that makes me fall right into a dream.
Whisper that you'll love me forever
and by my side, you'll stay forever.

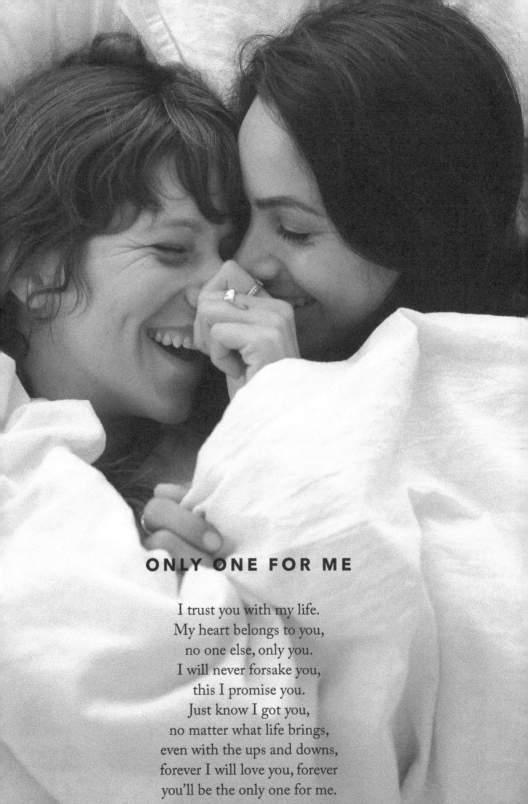

ONLY ONE FOR ME

I trust you with my life.
My heart belongs to you,
no one else, only you.
I will never forsake you,
this I promise you.
Just know I got you,
no matter what life brings,
even with the ups and downs,
forever I will love you, forever
you'll be the only one for me.

CRAZY OVER YOU

I'm crazy over you, my intentions are pure this is true. Every time you walk, your scent lingers everywhere, and this makes my mind think of you. Crazy over you, don't you know you are everything I wanted from day one, please don't ever leave my side because I'm crazy about you.

REASSURE ME

Reassure me I'm yours forever, don't let other girls think they can take you ever. Reassure me you are mine to keep, don't ever make that mistake you're not here to stay. Reassure me, I don't need to compete. You don't even see them and that's so sweet. Reassure me your love is true because I don't want to waste my love and time and that's not right. Reassure me you'll stay by my side because as long as you got me you don't need anyone else.

ACTING DIFFERENT

A stranger you are, definitely not the one you used to be,
you don't treat me the same way like when we first met.
Distant, it's clear to see you are acting very differently.
Could it be that you found someone different?
I hope this isn't true because it will surely break my heart.

THE ONE

I wanted you so much but you only like my body,
you didn't like me like that and that was that.
For me, you were the one, everything I was looking for and wanted.
It's too bad you never tried to get to know me the way I am.
So kind and sweet, yes, I am.
I wish you took a chance to see who I am.
The one for me, but not for you. It's so sad I can't have you.
If only I could be the one for you.
So, I guess I can only dream on that one.

EMPTY

Empty, it's not real, he doesn't see me the same way.
Empty, my heart is torn because there is no love to fill it in.
Empty, without you, I wish you could love me the same way.
Empty, my heart will be, as long as you're not in it.

BROKEN

My heart is broken to pieces.
Revive me with your love, your kisses, your hugs,
bring me back to life from this broken heart.
Let me never have to experience such heartaches and pain.
Let your love run over like a river that flows to my heart.
Love me like no other and heal this broken heart.

SILLY

Silly me thinking you would change,
how could I be so silly to fall in love,
with someone who doesn't even love me back.
Silly me believing that you loved me,
when all the signs were there.
Silly me for still forgiving you
every time you told me you were sorry.
Silly me, oh silly me for making you
steal my heart and then breaking it.
Shattered glass if only you can see it.
Silly me, thinking you were the one for me,
oh what a mistake I played myself.
Silly me, oh silly me if only if this was a dream,
so I can wake up from this horrible dream.
Silly me but this I know,
no one will ever get to break this shattered heart.
Silly me, oh never I be this silly me.

TRUST ISSUES

I got trust issues for all the lies you told me.
I got trust issues for all the misleadings you did.
I got trust issues for all the pains you put me through
and all those sleepless nights.
I got trust issues of you cheating with someone else,
while I was faithful to you.
I got trust issues of you telling me you love me,
when you never really meant it, because if you did,
I wouldn't have trust issues.

SOMEONE

When you have that someone
who gives you the support you need.
it's awesome to have someone who sticks with you
and pushes you to do your best
and who never gives up on you.
Someone to talk to and comfort you.
Now that's a keeper no matter what.

LET THEIR ACTIONS
SHOW YOU

You know when someone is into you,
not a day won't go by without them
reaching out to you, checking up on you,
wanting to hang with you, and spending
some time with you. Thinking of you
throughout the day, can't wait till they
see you again. Oh yes then you know if
they are really into you.

MIND

Your mind so great, your mind so smart, teach me how to be like you. So intelligent with the words that come out of your mouth, oh it could make me fall into a spell. So seductive, so refine you are so fine. Sometimes I feel like I'm in a dream. I pinch myself just to check. You make me feel so good about myself and that makes me confident. I could listen to you talk all day because your voice sounds like melody. You make my day so blessed.

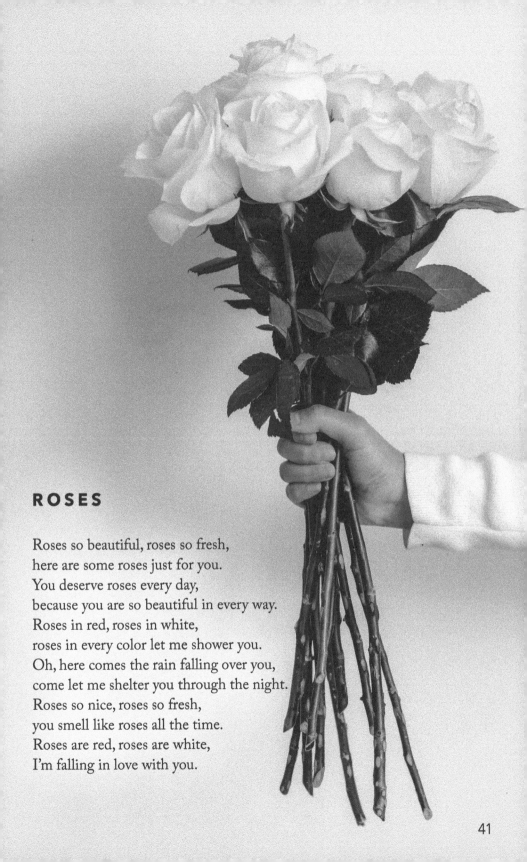

ROSES

Roses so beautiful, roses so fresh,
here are some roses just for you.
You deserve roses every day,
because you are so beautiful in every way.
Roses in red, roses in white,
roses in every color let me shower you.
Oh, here comes the rain falling over you,
come let me shelter you through the night.
Roses so nice, roses so fresh,
you smell like roses all the time.
Roses are red, roses are white,
I'm falling in love with you.

CHEMISTRY

Chemistry, I can feel it running through my veins,
the way you make me feel like no one else,
I can't explain this feeling surreal,
when I'm with you, I see no one else.
No worries, no stress in my head
as long as we're together I don't need anyone else.

MOTIVATE ME

Motivate me to be the best I can be,
motivate me to bring out the best in you.
Motivate me to push forward
even though it seems like there is no hope.
Motivate me to stay strong and proud no matter what.
Motivate me not to worry about anything in this world
because no matter what happens, you'll be there to motivate me.

HAPPY

Happy, happy I'll always be, for once your presence is here, I'll always be. Happy, happy it's good to find someone that makes me happy and brings out the best in me. Happy, happy I'm so pleased to make you happy and that will always be. Happy, happy you are mine; I'll keep you forever close to me. Happy, happy I love you and I'm so glad you feel the same way too.

WAITING

Waiting for you, where ever you are,
waiting for that right person to scoop you off your feet.
Waiting for that person to treat you like a King /Queen,
meaning, cherish and respect you, that's the way it should be.
Waiting for their love and their tender arm so sweet,
waiting, wondering when that will be.
Could be forever, oh no; don't let it be.
Waiting for them, just don't let it be forever.

WONDERLAND

I'm in wonderland thinking this was it,
thinking you were the one for me.
Thinking after all that you will change for me.
In wonderland, it's all a dream,
he definitely is not for me.
He only wanted one thing, you see.
I will not settle for that; no not me.
So, I guess I will stay in wonderland,
until I find the right one for me
and wake up from this horrible dream.

WHERE ARE YOU

Where are you my heart divine? I'm tired of waiting, could it be never. Oh, how I wish you could walk through the door, so I can stop searching for you and can't find you ever. Oh, how it hurts to watch them in love but for me never. Waiting for you, oh could this be that in my heart I won't find you ever. Please come and find me before it's too late, and I drown hopelessly without your love.

LOVE

Love such a beautiful thing.
Someone who loves you till the
end. Who would never forsake
you not ever, who knows your
flaws, and still, will keep you
forever, who'll stay with you
through the rough times, and
love you through it all. Love is so
wonderful, it's a beautiful thing,
so if you found it, don't let it go
because it's better to experience
it than to never had it.

DAY DREAMING

Daydreaming about you. Daydreaming about when we just met, how you were so sweet and did everything to make sure I was happy. You treat me like a queen. Open doors for me, take me everywhere because you love being by my side. You wanted to please me in every single way. Thinking about how you said, I was a dream come through. Now look at you the guy of my dreams who I thought was so great. Turned out to be a nightmare from sweet to sour, making me wish I never met you and the only thing I can do is daydream of what we used to be, oh bittersweet.

STOP

Stop breaking your own heart, if he was interested, he would call, he would text, not just once in a blue moon to stay relevant. He would want to spend time with you. He would show more interest if he is really into you. Stop ignoring these red flags. Please don't settle for these all, here and there, or just to meet up once in a while because he knows exactly who he wants and it's not you.

BETRAYAL

Trusted you with my life, trusted you with anything and everything I have. My heart, my lungs even with the air I breathe. I gave you my heart and I didn't hold anything back. My energy, my time I can never get that back. One lesson I learned from that I will never give anyone all of me until I know for sure that they love me for real and that's a fact.

WASTED TIME

Wasted time I can never get back.
Hey, you, with your style, looking so fly.
Stop leading me on, you're good at that.
So, stop with your games and all.
This minute you're into me, next minute you're not.
Hello, stop telling me you miss me so I can fall into your trap.
I'm done with lies, do you think this is a game?
If you didn't want my love, you should have said that.
Then after your lies and all of that,
my soft heart keeps taking you back, but I've decided.
I'm done with your games, and all of that
because I deserve someone better who would never do me that.
Selflove.

RUSH

Rushing into something new,
thought I was over you.
Memories keep rushing to my brain,
thinking about the good times we used to share.
Oh, the past lingers near,
waiting for it to disappear.
Then I realized you weren't the one for me,
no matter how hard I try.
I deserve someone so much better,
who will treat me so much better,
because you were never it.

FAITHFUL

A faithful person,
someone who would never mislead you.
Someone, who, you would never have to question their loyalty.
No lies, no games, truthful to you and will never deceive you.
Someone who got you to the very end.

REALIZING

When are you going to realize that you got it all?
A beautiful and faithful woman.
Who is always there to catch you when you fall.
Taking you back over and over again.
This heart is wounded with scars, lies, lies that's who you are. Telling
me you love me, oh what a laugh, showing me how evil you are and
breaking my heart.
I'm so done with you.
I know I said this before,
But this time I promise this is true.

GIVE UP

I give up, those are the words she says.
She was tired of chasing him.
He had told her once that she is just not good enough for him.
He wanted someone who is making all that money
and she is just not wealthy enough for him.
He was attracted to her physically but that wasn't enough for him.
She said I give up, he is not into me.
I said he doesn't love you for who you are.
He wants someone for their money and that's not going to go far.
Whoever he ends up with, both are not going to be right for each other,
because relationship is not all about money.
You need someone who is genuinely in love with you.
Who will be there no matter what.
I said you know what, it's his loss, not yours.
You deserve someone who will be there for you through the worse.
Even if you only have a little to give,
they will support and love you to the end.
So don't ever chase that guy,
you deserve that right person who will never leave your side.

COMING BACK

Coming back, he said, disappear, let her cool down, I'll leave her alone, he said. She'll just forget what I did. Give her time and then I'll pop up and see if she'll understand. You see she'll never find someone like me, not at all, he thought. She'll come to her senses and see I am all. She better put-up with all my crap, so what if I come in late or not at all. I'm all she got, she can't make it without me, that's what he thought. She put up with all of his lies and his negative ways, then one day she snaps and said I deserve so much better, I'm tired of his games. I know my worth now and you don't deserve someone like me. Never that. So, she left him and never went back and now she found someone who treats her like a queen with so much respect. She came to her senses and is living so happy after all she went through and all of that.

BROKEN HEARTS

To all the broken hearts,
your heart will heal again,
they weren't the one for you,
God saw it fit to remove them from your life,
Because you're a precious gem,
and you deserve someone better,
Someone who will love you dearly
and cherish you every day,
because you are worth more
than a diamond that shines so bright within.
So, wipe those beautiful eyes
and keep those tears away,
because your heart will heal again,
and God will send someone perfect,
who is beautiful inside out,
then you'll realize,
why your heart was meant to be broken
so you can find your special one.

MY HEART IS BROKEN

Why you got to break my heart. I didn't deserve that. I was nice and loving to you, but you still crush my heart so hard. I always had your back. I thought you said you loved me, so why did you do that? Oh, how can you love me if you're doing that to me? My heart is broken, don't you see? I can't even eat or sleep, why am I crying over you? I wish I could turn back the hands of time, so I can erase you from my memories. I wish I never met you. If only I could change that.

RELIEF

What a relief,
my heart hurts no more,
no more lies and betrayal,
oh what a relief.
What a relief to go to bed
with so much peace.
It's such a great feeling
to feel stress free.
No one to break my heart so fragile.
Now I feel so relieved,
and now I can be at peace.

TAKEN YOU BACK

Taken you back, oh no you don't deserve that. After all the stress you caused me, oh no I would never do that. Goodbye to you and all of your games. I'm done with you and that's that. Stop calling my phone and knocking on my doors. This is the finale and the end of the race, you had your chance, and you blew it and you aren't getting it back.

YOU ARE
WORTH IT

You are everything, that someone would want to have. Don't let anyone make you feel like you're not good enough. Don't let anyone tell you, you can't find anyone better than them. Don't let anyone treat you a certain way and mistreat you or try to lower your self-esteem. You are everything and more, always remember your worth and keep your confidence intact.

THE RIGHT ONE

Stop looking, the moment you stop searching for Mr. Right, that's when it will happen. I know you tried a million times, and it hasn't been working out. Just stop looking. Go out, socialize, and meet people. Do not force anything, the right one will show up just in time for the celebration. The celebration of happiness and comfort. Someone who got your back through the good and bad. Faithful and loyal, what a celebration! Relax and just wait for your celebration. It just needs some preparation and planning but get ready for it. Your celebration of Mr. Right is in motion, just wait for your turn.

OUT OF ANGER

He was mad.
He said things he never meant,
that were wrong out of anger.
Out of anger he hurt her heart.
The things he said wasn't right
and now she is feeling broken.
Out of anger, please don't say something
that will break someone's heart,
it's best to just walk away
and cool yourself down.
So, when you're upset and very angry,
just always be careful what you say
and never do it out of anger.

CHANGE

You can't change someone.
They got to be willing to change.
If they think you are worth it,
they will put out effort to change their ways
because they don't want to lose you.
Especially if they love you,
they will try their best to change for you,
but you can never force someone to change
because they have to want to do it willingly.

TIME

There is a time for laughing,
time for crying,
time for joy,
time for war,
time for peace,
time for you,
time for friends,
time for love,
time for break ups
and meeting someone else.
Time for mourning,
time for rejoicing,
time to enjoy yourself
and not waiting for someone else.

MINDSET

Focus on great things, worry less, I know the
stresses of life make you upset, try to stay positive.
I know sometimes it's hard to do, especially when
life is beating you down, but look to your father,
who is sitting up high. Trust me, he is watching
your every move. He will make sure that you're ok.
So, stick to the positive and throw out the negative
thoughts, because everything will be ok.

FOCUS

Focus on yourself, your happiness, your inspiration, your goals, your opportunity, your life. Choose to be happy, choose to enjoy every single day of your life. Live your life knowing you enjoy every bit of it. Live your life to the fullest.

APPRECIATE YOURSELF

I learn to appreciate myself more when I am alone, and I realize, I need nobody else. I had to go through stuff alone to realize I am strong, and I should never give up on myself. I learn to appreciate life more because once it's gone, it's gone forever.

HUMBLENESS

Humbleness, keyword, when you're on top, don't look down on others like you're better than them. Life is funny and karma can be a bitch and humble you really quick. Stay humble. Don't forget where you came from and who stand by you.

YOU ARE PRECIOUS

If only you knew how special you are,
you will never come across negative thoughts.
You are worth everything that's good,
don't let anyone tell you less.
You're like a star that shines so bright,
you light up the room when you walk in.
Your smile is so beautiful,
it makes them take a second glance.
It doesn't take much for people to see
how beautiful you are within.
So, don't you ever doubt yourself, neither you ever
let negativity get in your thoughts,
remember how precious you are.
Keep on loving yourself
and never doubt how good you are.

WHAT A HEART

What a heart, so loving and always looking out for people and making sure they are ok, and if not, you're the one always giving a helping hand. It's so good to have people in this world who are genuine with pure hearts, always helping those in need. Continue to be just the way you are, because in due time you will receive your blessing.

DON'T FORCE IT

I squash the beef, I said. Meaning, we don't have to be friends but since we see each other every day, let's just be casual. Ok, she said. Next day, I said hi, she shook her head, meaning, hi. Next time I saw her, she acted like she didn't see me, and so I thought, no matter how you try to be a better person, there is always going to be someone, who will dislike you. What you need to do is live your life the best you can, and treat people the best you can, do not force yourself to talk to someone if they do not want to talk to you nor they want to have something to do with you. Be around with people who treat you well. Be happy and live a stress free life.

CLEAN HEART

It's good to have a clean heart.
You should respect and treat people right.
Don't ever try to do people wrong,
because it will come back around
and you're not going to like it.

Be good to people, it's the best thing you could do,
then you will see the blessings coming your way.
Leave the people who do you wrong to God,
and keep on being good because your blessings will come.

STAND IN FRONT OF THE MIRROR

And say this:

I am strong,

I am amazing,

I am loved,

I will be fine,

I got this,

I will overcome all obstacles that come my way.

I will succeed,

I will be happy,

I am brave,

I am worthy,

I am everything God wants me to be,

no evil,

no envy,

no stress,

no financial difficulties will come my way

because I am covered by the almighty God in Jesus' name.

I am awesome,

I am a winner.

LET THE FEELINGS FLOW

Let it flow like a river, the feelings you feel so
deep within, feeling of doubt, feeling you can't
make it, feeling like giving up. Let it continue
to flow, and don't go back. I want you to stay
on land and know you can make it, you deserve
to be happy. There isn't a space for giving up
because you will make it. Believe in yourself,
have confidence in yourself, and never give up.

STRESSFUL THINKING

It's like you're having an exam at school, you're nervous, your heart rate goes up, and it feels like your heart is going to pop out of your chest. Your stress level elevates, you start to have a headache, your tummy feels like bubbles going up and down. Then your heart starts racing like you're running a hundred meters on the track. Your body starts to feel weak, and all you want to do is sleep. Your mind has a hundred floating thoughts. Stop, relax, take a deep breath, calm down, don't be so stressed. Life has a way of working things out. It may be windy for now but soon the sun will come out.

DEPRESSION

Hey, you are thinking you're all alone, thinking no one cares, thinking no one will miss you if you're gone, thinking you can't make it. Stop! Listen to me, you are loved, and you will be ok. Your family and friends care for you. You can make it and will beat this. Do not worry about what people think of you, you are you, and don't change. Give yourself a hug. You will be ok, keep your head up and don't bring yourself down. You are unique, cheer up my friend, this won't last forever, be patient and be kind to yourself, everyone makes mistakes.

ANXIETY

When you get this racing anxious feeling that makes you think a lot. Thinking of this, thinking of that. Omg! Just let it stop. Feeling stressed, so overwhelmed, and anxious is just half of it. Relax, be calmed, just don't you snap, just go and play some relaxing songs. Do not worry. Overthinking is not going to help, it only makes it worst. It is ok, it will stop just go to the happy place in your head because that will surely help because you don't want a nervous breakdown. So, when you feel like you're feeling stressed out, relax your mind and find your way out.

OVER

I thought this feeling was over, but it keeps
coming back. Go away, I said in my head, I'm
done with this, please, please just let it stop. I
try to calm myself down, but nothing helps.
This makes me feel so sad, I just don't know
what to do. I wish this feeling could go away
and never return again. I try to play music to
relax my mind and also try to take a nap, but
nothing seems to work. Seems like I got a lot
on my mind. I tell myself to relax but it looks
like my anxiety is taking the best of me.
Please let it stop.

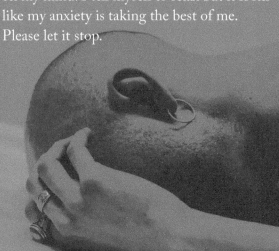

SITUATION

When a situation comes up, try to stay calm and think about the best way to solve the situation. Please don't stress yourself out, it will only cause you more harm than good. Calmness and taking control is the best way to go. Trust in your father up above, he will always listen to your call and be there to catch you if you fall.

KEEP PRESSING

Trapped in a closet, where to go, deep thoughts and stress
are wearing you out. Stop and think before you make a
move because you'll end up making the wrong move. Life
isn't easy, yes, it's hard, but you got to keep on pressing even
though it's hard. You can make it if you try. Just keep on
pressing, you'll make it through, this I promise you.

STRESS

They say it kills you faster. Stress is no good. It hurts you on the inside and shows on the outside. Stress is caused by numerous things, it could be from bad break-ups, losing a job, financial difficulties, losing a loved one, and more. It grows you weary. It makes you want to tie yourself up. It won't make you fall asleep at night. It also makes you demotivated, it could really drag you down. Stress makes you worry a lot. It really does a number on you. Try to beat it and never doubt that you can, because nothing is impossible. Please go around with loved ones who bring out the best in you. Also, be around with positive people who encourage you and motivate you. Take baby steps to solve your problem and also stay positive because that's a plus and know things will work out. Say a prayer every day and ask God to help you in every way. He will help, so don't you worry. Don't let things bother you so much. No need to work yourself out. Please try to do what is best for you and be stress free, so you can live a happier and healthier life.

DO WHAT'S BEST FOR YOU

Focus on yourself, focus on your happiness,
your inspiration, your goals, your opportunities, your life.
Choose to be happy, choose to enjoy every single day of your life.
Choose to be the best you can be.
Live your life knowing you enjoy every bit of it.
You own your destiny, you are what you make it.

Do what you love to do.
If you love to dress up and do your make up, do it.
If you love to go out, socialize and dance, do it.
If you love to go out and eat, just do it.
If you love to sing, do it.
Do whatever makes you happy.

FRUSTRATION

We all experience it. Sometimes frustrated with things not going
your way, but you must always have faith that things will work
themselves out. So, when you're frustrated, don't get too upset,
just keep pushing, you will make it out.

GENUINE

Genuine is truly defined as authentic and real. That's hard to find, someone you could turn to and lean on. Someone who won't betray you. Someone who genuinely cares and wouldn't do anything to jeopardize your trust. Genuine, a heart, so pure and real but all you can do is dream, hoping one day you'll find someone so real.

REALITY CHECK

Reality check, everyone will go one day, you know what I mean.
Reality check, don't trust anyone.
Reality check, even your closest friend can secretly wish you bad.
Reality check, people pretend well, so be careful.
Reality check, the truth always comes to reality.
Reality check, not everyone who says they love you, actually does.
Reality check, trust your instinct.
Reality check, care about yourself first because all you got in the end is you.

UNREAL FRIENDS

Had to let them go. I got love for you they say, but deep in their thoughts they don't wish you well and want to see you fail. The envy and the jealousy they have inside. Their thoughts you can't tell. God knows their thoughts, they pretend well. So, He had to let them go. You ever wonder how you had friends that disappear out of your life. God was hearing their thoughts and he had to protect you because they really don't want to see you win, and He had to let them go.

_Pray.
Trust.
Wait._

DON'T BE DISCOURAGED

Sometimes, you're happy, sometimes you're sad,
life has a way of putting you down,
put the stress and all your worries away,
you just got to give thanks for all you've got,
Once you get to the greatest peak of your life,
things will get better, just give it time.
No one is perfect, always remember that.

DON'T LOSE HOPE

Sometimes you will wake up and feel sad for no reason.
You're not even depressed, but these feelings just come over.
It happens to the best of us.
Cheer up, try to smile, and make yourself feel better.
Go to places that make you happy. Find things to do.
Hang out with friends and people that
make you feel good.
Think positive and just know that you are blessed and you got life.
Always try to make yourself feel better as much as you can.

LONELINESS

Some may experience it, some may not. What you need to know is, you came into this world alone, and you, in this world will leave alone. Learn how to appreciate yourself and appreciate others who appreciate you, learn to love your family even when they mess up. Acknowledge your worth and live by it, learn that sometimes you will fall, but you have to get up and move forward. Learn to know that not everyone is with you, and even your friends can betray you. Learn how to distinguish genuine from unauthentic. Trust that little voice in your head, it's called your instinct, and most of the time it's right. Always keep your head up, no matter how strong the storm seems, as they say, this too shall pass. Most importantly, love and take care of yourself, because yourself is your real bestfriend. Also remember, you are incomparable. Come through, because you got this all the way.

CHASING DREAMS

Don't be afraid, go chase your dreams.
Don't let anyone tell you, you can't do it,
because you sure can.
Don't be afraid to be the best you can be.

DON'T GIVE UP

Sometimes you feel like giving up.
Feeling down like there is no hope.
Thinking you're trying this hard and it's
not working out. So tired of pushing and
waiting for the day you see the colorful
rainbow. Wondering if you will make it
out of this stress you feel most of the time.
Think positive and just know things work
out just when you start to give up. So, keep
your head up and know things will work
out, just wait and see. Try to stay positive
and have faith, God will hear your cry.
Try to lift yourself up and stay strong.
Don't ever give up on yourself.

GET UP

When you had hit the worse, you got to get up.
Do not feel sorry for yourself.
Get up and overcome whatever you're going through.
Believe and try your best to never go back there.
Lesson learned. An experience you don't want to go back to.
Learn from your mistakes and never try to repeat them.

JUST IN TIME

Be patient in everything you do. Be patient, you will get there at the right time when you are supposed to. Don't rush, take your time, whatever is meant for you, you will receive. No need to worry about how you're not where you're supposed to be. Everyone has their own destiny. It is written, so be patient and wait for your time. Don't worry about, oh I'm getting old, I don't have kids yet. If your meant to have kids, you will. Don't worry that you haven't found your husband or wife. They say good things come to those who wait, and everything happens at the right time and place, you will get there just in time.

I MISS YOU

I remember one day I was crying, so sad, and feeling destroyed. You came up to me and said, wipe those tears from your eyes, it will hurt now but this too shall pass. Bad things happen to people, but it's how we overcome that terrible path. Be strong, just go to the door that leads you to a better path. Always have faith in whatever you do, believe there is nothing too mighty for you, as long as you get up if you fall, and learn from your mistakes. You will surely make it to the right path. Thank you I said, I feel much better. Now I'm here remembering those kind words you said but you're not here and this is sad. I miss you so much, I can't believe this is real. I hope you are watching down on me and I'm making you proud.

GONE

Gone forever, please tell me it's not true.
How could it be that I will never see you again forever?
Gone like the wind, I could only feel, but your presence I can't see.
Gone forever, don't let it be, just wake up and let me see.
Gone forever, please don't go.
I'll love you always,
I miss you forever.

THINKING OF YOU

Thinking of you, even though you're gone.
Thinking of all the good times we shared.
Thinking of how you always made me smile.
Thinking of how strong you were till the end.
Thinking of how I'm missing you so much and it makes me sad.
Thinking of you always, although I know you're here in spirit watching
   over me.
Thinking of you, because you'll always hold a special place in my heart.
Thinking how I will always love you even though you're gone.

AFRAID

Don't be afraid to tell someone you love them,
you might not get a chance to do it again.
Don't be afraid to love again. Your heart was broken but next time around,
you will find true love.

Don't be afraid to forgive, Jesus did it and so can you.
You don't have to be friends but at least your mind can be at peace.

Don't be afraid to let go of something that meant you no good.
You got to think of yourself because you come first.

Don't be afraid to go for your dreams,
don't let anyone tell you, you can't do it, because you sure can.

WISHFUL THINKING

Wishing you were here, so I can lay upon your chest.
Wishing you were mine till the end of time.
Wishing you would love me and stay by my side forever.
Wishing I could change what happened and go back in time
and fix everything. That would be so clever.
Wishing things could work, so, I can have you here with me forever.

FOREVER IN MY HEART

Missing you now and forever,
because you are special in every way.
Missing your hugs and your beautiful smile,
because it is one of a kind.
Missing you always, my heart aches, yes it does,
because when I think of you it makes me sad.
Missing your presence and all the things we used to do.
Missing you now and always in my thoughts.
Oh, how I miss you!

RETURN

I want you to return,
I miss you so much.
I miss your presence.
Return if possible,
but we all know that it is impossible.
Wish I could see you, touch you,
hold you, give you one big hug
and tell you how much I love you.
I know you're watching over me
each and every day.
But I just can't see you physically.
I know your spirit lingers nearby.
I just want you to know,
I miss you very dearly
and will continue to make you proud.

HERO

A hero, you are.
Can't you see how proud
we will always be of you?
You sacrificed your own life
just to save us.
We can never repay you.
A hero, you will always be,
and we will never ever forget you.
We will always remember
your brave and kind acts.
Forgetting yourself
and caring for others.
Always in our heart,
forgetting you never.
The bravest of them all,
you'll always be forever.

TRUE FRIENDS

Know who your true friends are.
They will be there for you when
you're at your lowest and feeling like giving up.
A friend who rides with you through the good
and bad to the end.
A friend, that even when you're not on good-terms
will not let your deepest secrets out.
A friend who knows when to leave you alone
and when to stay.
A friend who is your friend
even when you're not around.
A friend who checks on you every
now and then to see if you're ok.
A friend, who, when they have reached the peak of their success
wants to bring you with them and not forget you.
A friend who values you the way you do.
A friend who loves and respects you.

BESTFRIENDS

Hey best friend, what would I do without you?
Always there when I needed a shoulder to cry on.
You've been there through good times and bad times,
the break ups and the romance of being in love.
You've been my go-to and someone I can always count on.
To talk to when I had a situation I wanted to talk about.
You've been there with me having fun and enjoying each other's company.
You are a friend who will not leave me suffering in any way.
Hey best friend, I will always have your back the way you always have mine.
Best friend forever who keeps all my secrets and would never let them out
even when we have ups and downs.
Hey best friend, always know I love you and appreciate our friendship,
because you are amazing and thank you for being the best friend ever.

RUMORS

Rumors everywhere.
Why are you so jealous?
Going around spreading all those rumors.
Telling things that aren't true because you want that person to look bad.

Rumors everywhere.
Why do you have to tell those lies?
Why are you so envious? So not true.
What are you going to gain from putting someone down?

Rumors! Won't you stop?
Because you know the truth will always come out,
and when it does, you'll look like the biggest liar ever.

Rumors! You were wrong.
You better stop forever.
How would you feel if someone did that to you?

Rumors! It's not right
and it always leads back to you.

Rumors! This is not true.
And now they found out that it's you
spreading all the rumors.

Rumors everywhere.
Now they don't trust you.

TRIALS

There will be trials.
People will test you and some will use you.
Trials, someone trying to break you,
to put you down to a level where you can't succeed.
You got to stand fast and push to the best of your ability
to overcome any obstacle that comes your way.
Most of all, stay positive and encourage yourself
that no matter what comes your way, you will prevail.

QUITTING

Quitting is not an option,
don't ever do that.
You got to keep moving,
do not hold yourself back.
Keep on going, you can make it.
Don't you stop, please don't quit,
keep on pushing, you're almost there.
Go all the way to the top.
Success awaits you, don't you ever stop.

UNDECIDED

The path you take in life is up to you.
You don't need anyone
to make decisions for you.
Make decisions on your own,
you know what is right and what is wrong.
People are going to always give you advice
on what is right for you,
but they aren't always right.
Be open to listen to what they have to say
but learn to make your own decision wisely
and choose what is best for you.

ANGER

Let it out, no need to carry it around.
Go somewhere and yell it out.
Don't let it tear you down.
Anger! Anger! Go ahead and scream.
I know you're mad, take a deep breath and calm yourself down.
Anger! Things happen, people are going to get you upset sometimes.
No need to be rough just relax, please don't do anything bad.
Anger! Anger! You will be ok. It's just for the moment,
things will work themselves out.

KARMA

Karma everywhere.
I hope you get yours
from head to toe,
because you were mean
and that's so sad.

I hope your karma
catches you now,
run as fast as you can.
Here comes karma
right behind your back,
you can try to run
as fast as you can
but you can never escape
what is planned.
Karma, karma everywhere
you deserve what is coming to you.
I hope you learned your lesson
now and never
treat someone wrong again.

FORGIVENESS

Learn to forgive like Jesus.

People are going to betray you, hurt you, manipulate you. I remember this lady, her husband wasn't faithful to her, and also mistreated her. But, after all, she forgave him. She files for divorce and everything. Someone asked her one day "Why did you forgive your husband after all he put you through?" She said, "If Jesus forgives us our sins, we should learn to forgive others too. I know I went through a lot, but I can't keep all the anger and pain bottled up inside of me. I'd rather be at peace in my mind. I forgave him as Jesus did for me and everyone."

I SURRENDER

Lift me up from this weary ways.
Take away my fears.
Let me be strong,
confident, and bold.
Help me stand for what is always right.
Restore my spirit from doubt,
knowing anything is possible once
I put my mind to it,
and my trust in you.
Let me not be afraid of anything,
not even my enemies.
Let me be brave in everything I do, Lord.

DECEITFUL

Round of applause to this one here.
He thought he could cheat his way to the top.
Whatever that comes so easy is easy to lose,
because you didn't put out the work.
Round of applause, I told you it's wrong
but you wanted to prove them wrong.
These people put out a lot of work
to make it where they're at, to mount to their success.
Now, look at you looking all sad,
because you got caught.
I hope next time you'll think twice before you cheat,
because it's always good to do right.

YOU DID IT

They thought you couldn't make it, they surely did.
You studied, you worked hard and here you are.
Congrats to you! You're climbing to success.
Oh how could they have doubted you, they thought you couldn't win.
Hurray! Hurray! We are so proud of you.
You really are a star, so amazed,
how you made it this far after all you've been through.
You really put your all in and you deserve all of them.
Congrats to you, you climbed the mountain and reached the top.
No obstacles could stop you even though they tried.
All the sleepless nights and tears you cried,
you thought of giving up but thank God you didn't. Congrats again.
Hurray! Hurray! You made it, continue to soar to the top.

SO PROUD OF YOU

If only he was here to see
the person you turned out to be.
You worked so hard to be the best you could be,
and he'll be proud of who you are today.
You deserve the success story.
Hurray! Oh how great! You did it
all by yourself.
Studying hard surely paid off.
Congrats to you! Don't be amazed,
you worked so hard to get it.
So proud of you, he'll also be,
even though he is not here to say it.

UNFAIR TREATMENT

You could tell who the favorite is,
don't worry, I'm not jealous. My mommy taught me better.
She taught me, what is mine will always be mine,
and not to worry, when it's my time, it will happen.
So, you could be the favorite, I won't be envious, not ever.
I know what's mine will come in time and trust me, I will be fine.

MYSTERY

Oh, what a mystery it will be,
because I'm not letting it out of my head.
What I'm thinking you'll never know
because it's a secret I can't tell.
If only you knew what I was thinking,
you will probably just leave me alone,
because of a mystery.
It will be a secret I can't tell.

MY BEAUTIFUL MOTHER

Forever you will be, the beautiful person you are to me.
Beautiful soul and a beautiful treasure
and I'll always hold you close to my heart.
I'll love you forever, this I know because you always loved me
 from the moment I was in your stomach.

So beautiful, you'll always be my beautiful mother,
I'll love you forever.

MOTHER

I appreciate you for all the pain you went through
to bring me into this world.

I appreciate all those nights, you stayed up late,
when I was a newborn, even when you were so tired
and really want to sleep.

I appreciate you for going so hard for me
and not putting yourself first,
because you want the best for me and put me first.

I appreciate you Mom for being my rock when no one else would.

I appreciate you for caring and always being there.

I appreciate everything you do.

I love you.

LIFE

Live your life the best you can, you only get one,
so do your best to enjoy it with all you've got.

Live with no worries about what people think
because what they think doesn't really matter.

Live and be happy and nothing else,
because all that counts is that, you got life.

Live and enjoy this beautiful world
and let no one break you down.

Live and be you and no one else,
continue to live the best you can.

MARRIAGE

Congrats to you,
you have found the one,
the one that makes you incredibly happy.

Congrats to you,
you are in love,
and you decide to make it happen.

Congrats to you,
you have vowed to love
and cherish this person for the rest of your life
and be by their side, through sickness and health.

Congrats to you,
you will always have someone to be with you,
who will always comfort you.

Congrats to you,
go celebrate, you found your soul mate.

Congrats to you,
because love always wins, just treasure it forever.

GOD LOVES YOU

He loves you and he always will,
He died to save us from our sins.
Why can't you see He loves you,
why can't you see how much you mean to Him.
Why can't you see He adores you, He loves you.
Why can't you see that He loves you.
He is preparing a place for us,
it's paradise and all He wants you to do
is to live right, be true, and love one another.

REAL LOVE

Love, where are you? I've been waiting for you to come true.
So I can hold and feel your love, so real, this is true.
Love of happiness and everything that makes it feel so good,
that makes others want to be in love too.
Love so pure that makes my heart beat every time I see you.
Love doesn't keep me waiting because if I don't have you
I'll feel lost without you.

LIFE IS A BEAUTIFUL THING

Oh! How great is it to be blessed to be in this world,
even though it's full of sins.

Beautiful world, yes it is.
I thank God for creating us because it is a beautiful thing.
Enjoy this world with every chance you get,
because it's a beautiful world. Just dive in.

Live and be free.
Live and be happy.
Learn to forgive.
Love as hard as you can.
Love your life because once you get those,
you have everything.

Lightning Source UK Ltd.
Milton Keynes UK
UKHW051009040422
401050UK00005B/12